Mamie B. Pugh
John 3:16

Encircled In

God's Love

Mamie B. Pugh
Nancy R. Kinch - Artwork

B^TC
Beyond The Clouds Publishing Co.

Published by
B^{T}C
Beyond the Clouds Publishing Co.
790 Ford Rd.
Charlotte CH, Virginia 23923

Cover design by Mamie B. Pugh
Cover and inside art by Nancy R. Kinch

Printed in the United States of America
PIP Printing of Lynchburg, Virginia

First Edition

ISBN 0-9725373-0-9

To God
Be
The Glory

Author's Acknowledgments

A special note of thanks to my daughter, Mary Alice Easter, who encouraged me from the beginning. When I needed her she was always there with her winning ways, her patience, kindness, love, and talents. She has given many long hours. Without her this book might not have been.

Thanks to my sister, Nancy R. Kinch, who, also, gave of her love, her time and talents. Her paintings have added color to enhance the beauty of "Encircled In God's Love".

Also, thanks to Linda Wrenn LaPradd, Marina Gopadze and Henry M. Fulcher for their very meaningful contribution.

My thanks to Rob Cristo and his staff at Statesmen Computers. They have been very helpful in many ways.

My thanks to PIP Printing for their help, patience, kindness and a job well done.

Table of Contents

My Reflections and Thanks

Thanks,
a small six-letter word to express
a heart full of love and appreciation
for a lifetime of wonders.
Thanks to my heavenly Father,
who has given me everything.
In my "walk of life" there have been
many wonderful, joyous, happy times,
many valleys to pass through
and many mountains to climb.
But always, just when I needed them,
there have been those times of quiet;
when only the stillness
could suffice my need for the moment:
when only then, could I hear God's command to
"Be still and know that I am God."
During those times
when encompassed in stillness,
I could but wonder - "How big is God?"
How big is His universe and its wonders,
His love, His mercy, His forgiveness, His grace?

That He hears and knows my every thought
is far beyond my understanding.
How awesome - how majestic is God!
How humbled and grateful am I.
Within that "wonder" are the many things -
the many people who have touched my life
in some very special way.
If you have ever said to me a kind word or
given a helping hand when needed –
if you have ever laughed with me
or said a word of cheer
or held my hand when the tears were flowing –
if you have ever prayed for me
and believed that God would answer –
if you have ever walked the second mile with me
when the first mile was just not enough –
if you have ever "just been there"
when I needed you,
then you are among those
to whom "my thanks" go out reverberantly.

Among those is my family.

Each one, in his or her own special way,

has been an inspiration and a helping hand.

God filled my cup to overflowing when He gave me

Cecil, my husband.

My memories are very precious.

We love people -

but love for our life's chosen one

is something very special.

Howard, June, Mary Alice, Abe, Ronnie, Carolyn,

and my grandchildren

have helped to make a dream come true.

Thank each of you

from the bottom of my heart.

For the privilege of penning these words

I'm very grateful.

They have come to me because of God's love.

May they bless all who read them and come to you

as an expression of His love for each of us.

Mamie Pugh

Loving Words
To Cherish

And To Hold

In Your Heart

"...God is Love

and he that dwelleth in love
dwelleth in God,
and God in him."
I John 4:16

Love is of God

What is love?
Who can say what love is?
Who can describe its fullest meaning?
Love, records the dictionary, is an affection,
friendship, kindness, tenderness, fondness.
Yes, it is all of these.
But do they portray the real -
the true meaning of love -
the incumbent feelings of the heart?
I believe love goes beyond all of these
into a realm beyond words -
into a feeling beyond comprehension -
into something that is beyond and above
our most vivid imagination.
For love is of God.
God is love.

And who can comprehend this in its fullest -
its magnitude?
Surely - not I.

Father, I kneel before You and pray
that out of Your wonderful storehouse of love
Christ will come and dwell in our hearts today,
that we might receive Your love
with open hearts and minds,
that we might walk in love and grow in faith,
that we might know how wide and long -
how high and deep is Your love,
for love encircles all who will obey.
In Jesus' name -
with thanksgiving and praise.
To God be the glory forever and ever.
Amen

In the Banner of God's Love

Beyond my understanding
Is the God who loves me so.
Beyond all comprehension
Are the gifts He does bestow.

The joys of life and living
And peace from up above
To know that I'm encircled
In the banner of His love.

"He brought me to the banqueting house,
and his banner over me was love."
Song of Solomon 2:4

The Potter of Love

As the potter with skill
Molds the vessels of clay,
Reshaping and molding
In his own special way;
So the potter of love
Molds the hearts made of sod,
And makes of them beauty
To the glory of God.

"The Lord is my strength and my shield;
my heart trusted in him,
and I am helped:
therefore my heart greatly rejoiceth;
and with my song will I praise him."
Psalm 28:7

Life's Weavings

Life's Weavings

A tapestry I'm weaving
With the threads of life each day.
I would make it beautiful
With tones so bright and gay,
But God the Master Weaver
Has a different plan in view;
Among the bright and cheery
Are the shades of dimmer hue.
Among the dull and gloomy
A bright one lends its glow
To overcast the shadow
Which the dull ones do bestow.

And so in life the threads diverse
Are part of God's design.
The happy blended with the sad
Do all of life entwine.
Each lending to the other
In their own so special ways
Will make a life of beauty
For God's glory and His praise.

"I will sing unto the Lord,
because he hath dealt bountifully with me."
Psalm 13:6

"Sing unto the Lord a new song..."
Isaiah 42:10

Listen

Listen to the bluebird sing
Its joyous song of mirth.
Hearken to the mockingbird
The songs throughout the earth.
The sounds of God's creation
Proclaim the glory of
The God who has created them -
A God of life and love.

"Therefore will I give thanks unto thee,
O Lord, ... and sing praises unto thy name."
Psalm 18:49

How Great God's Love

God's love abounds in everything
It lingers everywhere -
From the tiny little dewdrop
To each wondrous gift so rare.
I see God's love in nature
As only He could give -
For who could make one seed to grow
Or make one life to live?
In the roses and the lilies
With their beauty to behold -
I'm reminded of His goodness
Of His love as pure as gold.

In each lively thing that blossoms
Each tall and towering tree -
I'm reminded of His greatness
How He made the land and sea.
When I see the cattle grazing
In the pasture - then I feel
The eye of our dear Shepherd
And I know His love is real.
As my family round me gathers
And their love I then do see -
I'm reminded how much greater is
God's love - than ours could ever be.

God speaks through His own.

Oh God, How Great

Oh God,
How great Your love
No one can comprehend -
That You are mindful of our needs
And did a Savior send.

Oh God,
How great Your mercy
I feel it everywhere -
Though You I cannot see or touch
I know that You are there.

Oh God,
How great Your faithfulness
That You will ever wait -
'Til these poor wandering hearts of ours
Will change before too late.

How great,
How great, oh God, You are
How great Your mercies be -
Our humble, longing, hopeful hearts
Can never fully see.

How great,
How great, oh God, You are.

This Thing Called Love

What is this thing called love?
Can its meaning we define?
Can we know how great its power?
Can we its force entwine?
Love's as a breeze that gently blows
To stir emotions from within -
And then it gains momentum
As the mighty raging wind.
We then can feel the force of it -
With joy our hearts will glow;
And though it is invisible -
It's meaning we will know.
Oh love - God's mighty force on earth -
Oh love - God's gift to man -
May we accept love graciously
Throughout life's pilgrim span.

Who Knows

Who knows but you may have planted the seed
That on fertile soil did grow,
And then did reap a harvest great -
Maybe you'll never know.
Who knows but that you
Might have said the word
That changed the course of someone
Who was traveling down the road of sin
Away from the light of home.
Who knows but that one little kind deed done
Even though it might have been small,
Did give forth hope to someone
Who from the heights did fall.
If planted today with the spirit of love,
Our deeds - though small may be,
Might bring forth bountiful harvest.
Who knows - but God will see.

Hope Renewed

Loving hearts and helping hands
Have carried me through life -
When then I could not walk alone
Mid turbulence and strife.
The hills I climbed were very steep -
The chilling winds - they blew -
But open arms and healing words
And God - did hope renew.

"Search me, O God, and know my heart:
try me, and know my thoughts:
And see if there be any wicked way in me,
and lead me in the way everlasting."
Psalm 139:23–24

Keep Me

I know not what may lie ahead
Or what's in store for me
What fortune or what blessings
Or what sorrow there might be;
But - Father - this one thing I ask
No matter what's ahead
May I ever humble be
And by your hand be led.
If fortune should so come my way
Or fame or great renown
May I remember that from You
These blessings have come down.

Help me to see that I am naught
Without Your guiding hand.
Without Your power within me
I'm but as drifting sand.
But with Your wisdom guiding me
I'll ever upward go
And onward to that Promised Land
Your love - Your love I'll know.

"Keep me as the apple of the eye,
hide me under the shadow of thy wings, ..."
Psalm 17:8

On Wings of Love

Sailing along on wings of love
I'll soar to heights unknown -
Searching for things of beauty
For treasures all my own.
While traveling to that city
That's made of purest gold -
I know I'll find the wonders
Of God's glory - yet untold.
For here we see so dimly
Through darkened glass - but then -
We'll see and know the wonder
Of God's plan that's now unseen.

"For now we see through a glass, darkly;
but then face to face: now I know in part;
but then shall I know even as also I am known."
I Corinthians 13:12

"How excellent is thy loving kindness,
O God! therefore the children of men
put their trust under the shadow of thy wings."
Psalm 36:7

"I will say of the Lord,
He is my refuge and my fortress: my God;
in him will I trust."
Psalm 91:1-2

"For he shall give his angels charge over thee,
to keep thee in all thy ways."
Psalm 91:11

Reach Up and Find

You'll find God's love in the rainbow
The raindrops showering down -
The sun with its warmth and brightness
Blue skies and clouds of down -
Uplifted hands of little ones
The words of comfort and cheer -
The light and hope of a new day
Aloneness holds no fear.
You'll find God's love in the tulips
The roses and lilies fair -
His hands reaching down from heaven
To give you His love and care.
His love reaching down in heartaches -
He's ever and always near -
Hoping and longing and waiting -
Reach up to His hand - have no fear.

Autumn's Message

Autumn's Message

In the early morning hours
I saw the shades of autumn's hue
The sparkling diamond dewdrops
The sky of purest blue
The shades of brown and yellow
The deepest, purest red
The orange in its splendor
Some on the ground were spread.
They spoke in nature's harmony
In praise so soft and low
They're giving of their beauty
God's glory to bestow.

The beauty of creation
Is a glory unto God.

Blessings

Count your blessings - look around -
The love of God is near.
In the sky the rainbow's beauty
Arcs above the earthly sphere.
The lilies clothed in splendor
The rose's fragrance true -
A dear one's joyous laughter
Love's glowing rays in view -
A world of awesome beauty
A chance your dreams to reach -
A helping hand to guide you
If only you beseech.
So look around - examine
What life gives forth today.
Look for your blessings many
So evident - for aye.

God clothes the lilies in beauty.
Shall He not much more clothe his children
in robes of white and
wrapped in cords of mercy?
God clothes the earth in color
And He fills our hearts with love.

Majestic In

Its Splendor

Majestic In Its Splendor

I cannot comprehend it
This love from God on high.
It reaches to the highest realm
From earth up to the sky.
From shore to shore - from sea to sea
We're basking in His love;
Majestic in its splendor
So wondrous from above.

God's Love
Unlimited, Unmeasurable,
Magnanimous

Our batting average of life
might well be determined
by dividing our willingness to try
into our smiles,
the kind words spoken,
the helping hands rendered,
the examples we have been
and the zest and the joy of our living.

Talents

Some may teach with words of ease
And fluent tongue each day.
Some may be good leaders
And spread cheer along the way.
Some may have the talent
To heal within their hand;
Others may have voices
Of beauty to command.
Whatever talent is our lot
Be it great or small;
God blessed us so that we might give
In answer to His call.
Each one has a life to give
To Satan or to God;
And the way we use our talents
Shows the path that we would trod.

Salvation's Robe

Lift up your eyes and look around -
And see God's glory there abound.
Then praise the Lord for all His might -
His love - His truth - He is the light.
The deaf shall hear - the bound be free.
The broken hearted - love shall see.
The ashes then will beauty be -
Salvation's robe - eternity.
God is the potter - we're the clay.
We are His work from day to day.
He takes our sin-filled lives and then
Gives beauty - where were the ashes of sin.

"... to give unto them beauty for ashes ...
that He might be glorified."
Isaiah 61:3

Life

A brimming cup of happiness
An apportioned lot of tears
A loving hand to guide us
And banish all our fears.
The sunshine after storm clouds
The rainbow in the sky
Heartache - then the laughter
As the days go drifting by.
A lot of good in each of us
To overcome the bad
The sweet bliss of success
If a failure we have had.
A friendly hand to help us
With our daily cares and strife
A God above to love us
This is wondrous life.

The gift of today's dawn
brings forth a new day
untarnished with 24 hours.
If God so chooses
to give me this day
I'll look into its sunrise
and know that
God is there,
and pledge it my best.

True Riches

No worldly riches do I crave
To make a glamorous show -
That earthly friends might flock around
And I their paths might go.
The riches that I long for
Are the ones I find in Him -
The ones that He will give me
If I will let Him in.
If I will let Him lead me
There's peace of mind and soul -
And wondrous things are given
When I enter in God's fold.

"Prove all things;
hold fast that which is good."
1 Thessalonians 5:21

"For what shall it profit a man,
if he shall gain the whole world,
and lose his own soul?"
Mark 8:36

"Lay not up for yourselves treasures upon earth,
where moth and rust doth corrupt,
and where thieves break through and steal:
But lay up for yourselves treasures in heaven,
where neither moth nor rust doth corrupt,
and where thieves do not break through nor steal:
For where your treasure is,
there will your heart be also."
Matthew 6:19-21

Out of the Heartache

Out of the heartache comes triumph
How can this be dear Lord?
By searching and seeking and longing
For comfort that comes from Your Word.
When through the valley I'm struggling
The way seems so dark - so drear.
Your promise of comfort and guidance
Your presence is ever so near.
And, yea, though I walk through the valley
My Shepherd will lead the way.
Green pastures are ever before me,
Still waters are on the way.
Yes, out of the heartache comes triumph
The victory from God - so divine
The joy and peace of His caring
To know that they surely are mine.

Choose Wisely

Choose Wisely

Today I held a tiny little hand in mine
And looked into two sparkling blue eyes.
I felt a tiny heart beating rhythmically
and I heard the sounds of laughter.
I saw a special kind of trust and love
that beamed from within.
So innocent - so precious - is a little child.
And I thought, "Dear precious one,
you have a long way to go.
This little hand will have many tasks to perform.
Your shining eyes will see the beauty
of God's creation around you.
They will also see the not so beautiful.
These little feet will walk many miles.
This little heart will beat many rhythms,
feel many emotions.
The pathway ahead is unknown,
unknown to one and all.

Life is a mystery.
You will have many questions.
You will wonder about many things.
Many choices will be yours to make.
As you grow
there will be facts and knowledge to learn
and wisdom to gain.
Knowledge is of the world.
Wisdom is from God.
Choose wisely.
In your choosing look for the beautiful.
Search for the truth. Long for the right.
Aspire to know the miracles of creation -
to know God.
Along the way there will be many roadblocks,
many rough places.
There will be heartaches and hurts.
Flee from temptation. Avoid the evil.

Through it all know that God is ever present,
all knowing, all powerful, and all loving.
If you should take a wrong turn
in the road of life - turn around.
Return to God and He will return to you.
Have no fear; He is with you.
In the good times and in the bad times
He is near. Trust Him.
When all others forsake you
and the clouds hang low - trust God.
Precious one, keep that sparkle in your eyes.
Laugh - even when laughing hurts.
Trust and believe -
And keep on trusting and believing.
Hang on to that last bit of hope.
Love when all love seems gone.
Nothing is too hard for our God to do.
He is ever ready to help you.
Choose wisely.

Seek faithfully, stand firmly,
Search diligently and you will find
A kind word, a helping hand, healing,
whatever may be your need.
Search and keep on searching. Look up.
Lift up your hands and receive.
Receive the peace, the joy, the love, the forgiveness,
the healing of mind, body and soul,
that only God can give.
The Shepherd watches over His lambs.
Choose to be one of His own.
The guardian of your soul is watching over you.
He is waiting with open arms
to give you the Way Everlasting -
His Way - His Love.
Precious little one - in all of life choose wisely.
God loves you and so do I."

Only He

Who can calm my troubled mind
And ease my aching heart?
Who can check the evil thoughts
Which Satan does impart?
I cannot find the strength
Within myself to fight the foe.
Only He can help me.
God's Grace He can bestow.
Who can help me see myself
For what is really there?
Who can break the arrogance -
The pride - the haughty air?
Only Christ who gave Himself
In service kind and true
Can help me so that God
Instead of Satan will shine through.

Who can save my wayward soul
From death and evil's lure?
Who can take my sinful heart
And make it white and pure?
Only He who took my guilt
And bore the blame for me
Can save me so that I
Might live eternally.

"Jesus saith unto him,
I am the way, the truth, and the life:
no man cometh unto the Father, but by me."
John 14:6

"He that hath an ear, let him hear what the Spirit
saith unto the churches; To him that overcometh will
I give to eat of the tree of life, which is in the midst of
the paradise of God."
Revelation 2:7

God Cares For His Own

No matter where His own might be
God watches o'er them - He can see
Their every need, their every care,
And He can hear their every prayer.
God had a plan for Abraham.
He led him on to Canaan land
To build of him a nation great -
And many blessings to emanate.
Though Joseph had a stormy path
He saw God's love instead of wrath.
And then through Moses God did lead
His children so they could be freed.
He gave them men to lead them on -
Daniel, Joshua and Solomon.

Elijah was a prophet great;
Elisha was compassionate.
And then the greatest of them all
One fully man and fully God
Came down to us from heaven above
To show the depth of God's great love.
He came to seek the lost - to save -
He with His life a ransom gave
To free those from the cord of sin
Who'll let the Savior reign within.
Down through the years
God's guiding hand
Has led His own in every land.
Great love He has so freely shown
God truly cares for each His own.

Precious Moments

The moments with Thee are precious
When I can be thankful for
The blessings which on earth are mine -
So many I've had in store.
When I can be thankful for Jesus
Who died on Calvary
That I might have life eternal
That I might from sin be free.
When I can cast every sorrow
And care on the shoulders of Him
Who ever longs to be with us
To make life's burdens dim.
When I can open my heart and pray
And know that God is there
And know that He will listen
And hear my every prayer.

Miracles

The miracles in the Bible
Are many and great indeed.
They tell us how our God above
Provides our every need.
One tells of the burning bush -
One the parting of the sea -
So God's children there could cross -
From bondage to be free.
God's miracles won many battles -
He stayed the moon and sun -
He raised the dead to life again -
He healed the blind and dumb.
But the greatest of God's miracles
Is the one that proved His love -
When He sent to us a Savior -
Who came down from heaven above.

He gave to us our freedom
From the bondages of sin.
He gave us life eternal
If we will let Him in.
Our wealth cannot buy entrance
To the gates of heaven's shore.
We cannot work or bribe our way
To get through heaven's door.
But Jesus opened wide the gate
When Calvary's cross He bore -
When on that cross He bled and died -
To live forevermore.
Yes, the greatest of God's miracles
Is the miracle of His love;
When He sent to us a Savior
That we might live with Him above.

Stairway of Prayer

How can I find life's deepest needs -
How can I these attain -
How can sweet peace and joy be mine -
How can God's love I gain?
Assurance surely can be mine -
I'll climb the stairway of prayer -
And with each step I'll nearer be
Within God's presence there.
For patience, love and joy I seek -
Sweet peace, God's gift divine -
Redemption through His grace is given
As step-by-step I climb.

The step of faith is there for me -
The healing of the soul -
Forgiveness comes along the way -
While climbing to the goal.
Each step I take I'll nearer be
To heaven's eternal bliss -
In prayer I'll find God's love divine -
Not one step will I miss.
The truth, the way will lead me on -
Obedient in my climb -
God's banner over me is love -
His peace and joy sublime.

"Call unto me, and I will answer thee,
and shew thee great and mighty things,
which thou knowest not."
Jeremiah 33:3

Where are the Nine?

On to Jerusalem the Master went
As He traveled so long ago.
He entered a certain village
As on the way He did go.
There in this village were lepers
Despised and feared by men.
"Have mercy on us Jesus, Master,
Have mercy," cried the lepers - ten.
"Go show yourselves to the priest", Jesus said,
"Go show yourselves, ye men."
And as they went the lepers were cleansed -
Those lepers - those lepers - ten.
And one - when he saw that he had been healed -
Turned back to thank Jesus - and praise.
He fell on his face at the Master's feet -
His voice of thanksgiving to raise.

"Were there not ten of you lepers cleansed?
But now, Oh where are the nine -
Where are the nine," the Master said,
"Oh where, oh where are the nine?"
"Arise," Jesus said to the faithful one,
"Thy faith hath made thee whole."
Oh what a blessing this one received -
The healing of heart and soul.
Now where, oh where am I today -
With the nine or the thankful one?
By His stripes I am healed,
my soul is redeemed
By the blood of God's crucified Son.
I thank Him, I praise Him,
as on bended knee
I cry to the Father above.
No less should I do, than to glorify Him
For His marvelous gift of love.

Untangle the Web

Untangle the web of my life dear Lord -
Untangle the wrongs I've done.
Untangle the thoughts of my mind dear Lord -
To focus - believe in Your Son.
Help me dear Lord as I walk life's way -
Guide every footstep - every day.
Strengthen and comfort - uphold I pray -
Walk with me Lord each step of the way.

"Serve the Lord with gladness:
come before his presence with singing."
Psalm 100:2

Go as a Witness

Go as a witness, our Savior said -
Go into all the world.
Proclaim the hope of redemption -
The power of God's word unfurl.
This great commission is given
To all who would stand so true.
God gave His Son to redeem us.
He now is depending on you.

"And he said unto them,
'Go ye into all the world,
and preach the gospel to every creature.
He that believeth and is baptized
shall be saved;' ..."
Mark 16:15-16

Oh Troubled Hearts

Let not your hearts be troubled -
Our Savior knows your needs -
He ever watches over you -
His Spirit intercedes.
When sometimes you are saddened
And often fall in doubt -
Remember - He has told us
That all things will work out.
All things will bring forth good
To those who love the Lord -
To those who put their trust in Him -
Believe His Holy Word.
When tempted then to question
What the answer there might be -
Remember - trouble not your heart -
But look God's love to see.

"Let not your heart be troubled:
ye believe in God, believe also in me.
In my Father's house are many mansions:
if it were not so, I would have told you.
I go to prepare a place for you.
And if I go and prepare a place for you,
I will come again, and receive you unto myself;
that where I am, there ye may be also."
John 14:1-3

"And we know that all things work together for
good to them that love God,
to them who are the called
according to his purpose."
Romans 8:28

God's Eternal Love

We'll Meet Again Come Dawn

Today a shadow crossed our path -
It took the form of death.
Death's angel plucked a blooming flower -
For him 'twas earth's last breath.
This flower of beauty here on earth
Now blooms on heaven's shore.
His life of love and radiance here
Now shines forevermore.
Though we with saddened hearts do grieve
Our tears so freely flow -
It should not be - for he lives on
His beauty still aglow.
His presence still is with us;
His memory lingers on.
Though absent for a little while -
We'll meet again - come dawn.

"And God shall wipe away all tears
from their eyes;
and there shall be no more death,
neither sorrow, nor crying,
neither shall there be any more pain:
for the former things are passed away."
Revelation 21:4

"My mouth shall speak the praise of the Lord:
and let all flesh bless his holy name
for ever and ever."
Psalm 145:21

When I Face Life's Setting Sun

When I face the setting sun
Of this life on earth below -
May I see its beauty shining -
May I know its radiant glow.
May I know it is the gateway
To Heaven up above -
To a better home with Jesus -
To a home that's filled with love.
May I never fear its coming -
When my race on earth is run -
For my Savior will still lead me
When I face life's setting sun.

"Preserve me, O God:
for in thee do I put my trust."
Psalm 16:1

"Thou wilt show me the path of life:
in thy presence is fullness of joy;
at thy right hand
there are pleasures for evermore."
Psalm 16:11

"But as it is written,
Eye hath not seen,
nor ear heard,
neither have entered
into the heart of man,
the things which God hath prepared
for them that love him."
I Corinthians 2:9

Somewhere in the Shadows

Standing somewhere in the shadows
Ever listening for our call -
Is our Savior who is watching
To protect us ere we fall.
His feet are staid - His hands are tied -
'Til we give Him the sign -
And ask Him to walk closer
That the light for us might shine.
He is waiting in the shadows -
He is ever lingering there -
To hear the faintest whisper -
Or to hear the silent prayer.
It takes no loud voice ringing -
But just a thought within -
To bring Him from the shadows -
That we might walk with Him.

"The Lord is good
unto them that wait for him,
to the soul that seeketh him."
Lamentations 3:25

"Wait on the Lord:
be of good courage,
and He shall strengthen thine heart:
wait, I say, on the Lord."
Psalm 27:14

"Commit thy way unto the Lord;
trust also in him;
and he shall bring it to pass.
And he shall bring forth
thy righteousness as the light,
and thy judgment as the noonday."
Psalm 37:5-6

The Rainbow

Oh rainbow, with your beauty rare -
Beaming in the sky so fair -
When once the storm has passed us by -
Remind us that our God is nigh.
Your beauty is a token of
A promise from our God above -
A promise made to Noah there -
And to his sons and wives so fair.
And to every living thing -
That on the ark He there did bring;
That by flood He'd never again
Destroy all on the earth's domain.

"I do set my bow in the cloud,
and it shall be for a token
of a covenant between me and the earth."
"And I will remember my covenant,
which is between me and you
and every living creature of all flesh;
and the waters shall no more
become a flood to destroy all flesh."
Genesis 9:13, 15

"Sing unto the Lord a new song..."
Isaiah 42:10

Your trial may be your greatest blessing.
Visualize the good it may bring forth.
Expect the best.

A Tiny Little Witness

A little girl was walking
By the prison gate one day -
She sang "Jesus Loves Me"
In the old familiar way.
There was a hardened criminal
Within the prison walls -
Though many tried to reach him
He resisted all their calls.
And then his heart was humbled
By this voice so soft and true -
It brought back to him memories
Of the mother's love he knew.
And how she used to sing
That same song to him then.
The tears, they started flowing -
For he realized his sin.

We know not when our actions
Or the words we say each day -
Might lead someone to Jesus -
Or in the path the other way.
This little girl there singing
Never knew that it was she -
Who saved this poor lost sinner
As she sang "Jesus Loves Me".

"Let the word of Christ
dwell in you richly in all wisdom;
teaching and admonishing one another
in psalms and hymns and spiritual songs,
singing with grace in your hearts to the Lord."
Colossians 3:16

Why

When we see broken bodies
Wracked with pain and care each day
And little children suffering -
Or a dear one called away -
We're tempted then to wonder
Why the pain and strife must be -
Why the innocent must suffer -
And the evil still be free.
The human minds within us
Ask these questions every day -
And yet we cannot understand
The mystery of God's way.
But He is watching o'er us
With a kind and loving eye -
And someday we will see the good -
And know the reason why.

The Brightest Light

Who is the truer witness -
What is the brighter light -
What stays with us the longest -
Which candle is more bright?
Is it the loud voice ringing -
Or the one who works the most -
Is it the eloquent speeches -
That tend to make us boast?
Sometimes our words are empty,
When they come not from the heart.
Our service could be rejected -
If haughtiness we impart.
But I think of the girl or lady
In all her humility -
Who quietly goes about loving -
And serving so willingly.

Or the boy or man who spends his time
In service kind and true -
Who does it with sincerity -
Never boasting to me and you.
We need the words to guide us -
And we need the service true -
But mostly the humble spirit -
Will make our witness shine through.

"Peace I leave with you,
my peace I give unto you:
not as the world giveth,
give I unto you.
Let not your heart be troubled,
neither let it be afraid."
John 14:27

In the Land of Tomorrow

In the land of all tomorrows
What will my future be
Will the family be reunited
Will I my loved ones see
Will I see my friends and neighbors
Will I walk the streets of gold
Will I sing God's hallelujahs
Will I heaven's glories behold
Will the arms of my Savior be open
Will His voice say "Welcome In"
Will I live in that beautiful city
Will I have a mansion therein?
Those who are meek and merciful
Who hunger and thirst each day
For the bread and water of life
Who believe in Christ and His way

Are included in "whosoever"
And that means you and me.
Whosoever will may come
Eternal life to see.
The mansions are many in heaven
Our Savior's preparing a place
For all who will believe in Him
Receive His saving grace.
For each who walks the Christ-like way
Will partake of the tree of life
And his name will be recorded
In that wonderful book of life.

"For God so loved the world,
that he gave his only begotten Son,
that whosoever believeth in him
should not perish, but have everlasting life."
John 3:16

Yesterday, Today, Tomorrow

Walking along life's memory lane -
Mementos of yesterday now to regain -
Looming are pictures so vivid, so clear -
Many fond memories this heart holds dear.
Are yesterday's musings today's regret -
Are yesterday's heartaches lingering yet -
I'll strive to remember - while pondering the past
The good things that happened -
the things that will last.
The heartaches I'll place in the hands of the one
Who came to redeem us that victory be won.
Yesterday's gone and today is for living -
For hoping and sharing - for loving and giving.
Whatever the time be allotted to me -
Whatever the time - God's gift may be -

'Tis given to serve - to love - and to care -
God's blessings on earth with others to share.
Our dear Savior's life was compassion filled.
'Twas given to do only that which God willed -
Loving and serving wherever the need -
Teaching and preaching and sowing God's seed.
We are His tongue, His hands and His feet
To teach and to serve - to go and to meet
The needs of His children - whatever they be.
Today is now given God's love to see.
Tomorrow - tomorrow - will I remain here
To live among those whom I love so dear -
Will I be allotted a forthcoming day -
Will tomorrow be mine to pilgrim the way?
Whatever it be, the assurance is mine
Of God's saving grace and His promise divine.

There's hope for tomorrow -
His promise is true.
His love He has given to me and to you.
Wherever I spend it - on earth or above -
I know it will be in the realm of God's love.
His hands are outstretched -
His arms open wide
To welcome those who in His love will abide.

"Ask, and it shall be given you;
seek, and ye shall find;
knock, and it shall be opened unto you:
For every one that asketh receiveth;
and he that seeketh findeth;
and to him that knocketh
it shall be opened."
Matthew 7:7-8

Diamonds are carved under pressure.
The carvings of my heart may well become
the diamonds of my soul.

The Perfect Love

The Perfect Love

A love that never ends,
A love divine
that fills our hearts to overflowing,
that reaches down to those
who lift their hands in praise.
God has given life.
He is the Creator of life.
But what is life without love,
pure love, true love?
Love is God's gift
to all who will receive.
God's Love, Divine Love.

*Faith is believing and knowing
that the ultimate good of our Creator's plan
is ours for the asking
and the reaching out to receive.*

Father

Our hearts are brimming over
with the wonder of the miracle of your love.
Our cups overflow with the happiness and joy
of being within your fold.
None other could give his own son:
to die that we might live -
to live that we might love -
to love that we might become
one in the family of God.
How blessed we are.
The hope and promise of every tomorrow -
whether it be on earth
or in the realm of heaven's glories -
is to know that surely we are
"Encircled in God's Love"
now - forever - and always.

Praise

and

Glory to God

Amen

Mamie B. Pugh was born in Charlotte County, Virginia. Her younger school days were spent in Cincinnati, Ohio and Covington, Kentucky. Until his homegoing in 1994 Mamie and her husband, Cecil, lived fifty-two years on the farm where she is now. They had two sons, Howard and Ronnie and one daughter, Mary Alice, all now grown and married. The writings in this book reveal the innermost emotions of one who feels that she is truly "Encircled in God's Love."

Nancy Kinch, Mamie's sister, did the beautiful paintings. She, too, is very thankful for this gift that God has given her. Nancy has one son, George, who lives in Brandy Station, Va. Her home is now in Richmond.

TO ORDER

ENCIRCLED IN GOD'S LOVE   (ISBN 0-9725373-0-9)

$8.95 per book .... I want _____Copies $_____
4.5% tax $_____
S&H $3.95 plus $1.50 each additional book $_____
                                                         TOTAL $_____

Send check or money order to:

Beyond the Clouds Publishing Co.
790 Ford Rd.
Charlotte Court House, VA 23923

Phone (434)542-5477

TO ORDER

ENCIRCLED IN GOD'S LOVE   (ISBN 0-9725373-0-9)

$8.95 per book .... I want _____Copies $_____
4.5% tax $_____
S&H $3.95 plus $1.50 each additional book $_____
                                                         TOTAL $_____

Send check or money order to:

Beyond the Clouds Publishing Co.
790 Ford Rd.
Charlotte Court House, VA 23923

Phone (434)542-5477